PREFACE

Lord Kevin's castle, although imaginary, is based in concept, structural process, and physical appearance on several castles built to aid in the conquest of Wales between 1277 and 1305. Their planning and construction epitomized over two centuries of military engineering accomplishments throughout Europe and the Holy Land.

The town of Aberwyvern, also imaginary, is based in concept and physical appearance on towns founded in conjunction with castles in Wales during the same twenty-eight-year period. This combination of castle and town in a military program displays both superior strategical skill and the farsightedness required for truly successful conquest.

⚜   ⚜   ⚜   ⚜   ⚜

CASTLE

CASTLE

DAVID MACAULAY

HOUGHTON MIFFLIN COMPANY BOSTON

To the past — farewell

ISBN: 0-395-25784-0 Reinforced Edition
ISBN: 0-395-32920-5 Sandpiper Paperbound Edition

Printed in the United States of America

RNF HOR PAP CRW 20 19 18 17 16

Library of Congress Cataloging in Publication Data

Macaulay, David.
  Castle.

  SUMMARY: Text and detailed drawings follow the
planning and construction of a "typical" castle and
adjoining town in thirteenth-century Wales.
  1. Castles —Juvenile literature. 2. Fortification —
Juvenile literature. [1. Castles. 2. Fortification]
I. Title.
UG405.M18   623'.19'429   77-7159
ISBN 0-395-25784-0

On March 27, 1283, King Edward I of England named Kevin le Strange to be Lord of Aberwyvern — a rich but rebellious area of northwest Wales. Although the title was bestowed out of gratitude for loyal service, the accompanying lands were not granted without a more significant royal motive. In an attempt to dominate the Welsh once and for all, Edward had embarked on an ambitious and very expensive program to build a series of castles and towns in strategic locations throughout the land. Whenever possible he encouraged loyal noblemen like Kevin to undertake, at their own expense, similar projects which would fit into his master plan.

Both castle and town were intended as tools of conquest but each had its own distinct function. The castle and the wall which was built around the town were primarily defensive structures.

Whatever offensive use they had stemmed from their placement along important supply and communication routes and to some extent from their intimidating appearance. Their most important function was to protect the new town. Once established and prosperous, the town would provide a variety of previously unavailable social and economic opportunities, not only to the English settlers who would first occupy it, but eventually to the Welsh as well. By gradually eliminating the need and desire for military confrontation a town, unlike a castle, would contribute to both conquest and peace.

In order to protect his newly acquired land, Lord Kevin immediately began making preparations to build both a castle and a town. He hired James of Babbington, a master engineer of great skill, to design the project and supervise the work. At King Edward's suggestion a site was to be selected along the coast near the mouth of the river Wyvern, a vital link between the mountainous interior and the sea. After considering several possibilities, Master James and his staff settled on the exact location.

The castle was to be built on a high limestone outcrop, which extended into the water. This took advantage of the natural defensive properties of the river and, at the same time, because of the height of the outcrop, assured an unbroken view of the adjacent land. At the foot of the outcrop, where the castle site was accessible from the land, he located the town. It would act as a landward barrier and together with the river would create the castle's first ring of defense.

In addition to his staff, Master James had brought with him diggers, carpenters, laborers, and several boatloads of timber, tools, and hardware.

The carpenters were immediately put to work erecting barracks and workshops for themselves and for the soldiers who would protect the site. They also constructed a large but still temporary building to house Master James and staff, as well as Lord Kevin and his family, who were expected sometime the following month.

Once the approximate perimeter of the town had been established, the diggers enclosed the area with a wide ditch. Carpenters then erected a sturdy wooden fence called a palisade along the inside edge of the ditch to secure the site until a more permanent stone wall could be constructed.

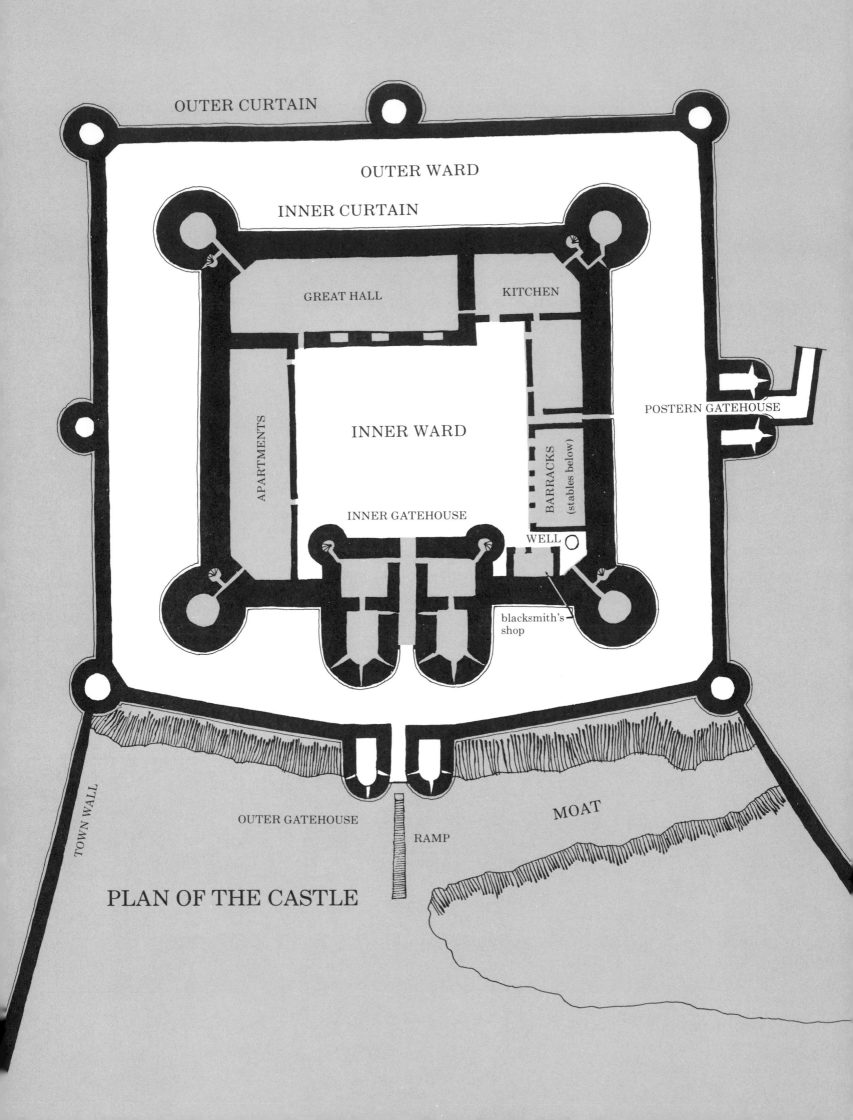

OUTER CURTAIN

OUTER WARD

INNER CURTAIN

GREAT HALL

KITCHEN

APARTMENTS

INNER WARD

BARRACKS (stables below)

POSTERN GATEHOUSE

INNER GATEHOUSE

WELL

blacksmith's shop

TOWN WALL

OUTER GATEHOUSE

RAMP

MOAT

PLAN OF THE CASTLE

As soon as the preliminary work was under way, Master James and his staff began planning the entire complex. The castle was designed first. The most important considerations were that it be able to resist direct attack and withstand a siege. This increasingly popular and often successful tactic involved surrounding both castle and town completely, cutting off all access to the outside. The strategy was simply to wait until all food and drink within the walls were gone, leaving the defenders with two equally unpleasant alternatives — starvation or surrender.

In planning the castle defenses, Master James combined several ideas developed in other castles, on which he had served as apprentice to the master engineer. The castle was laid out as a series of progressively smaller yet stronger defensive rings, one inside the other.

The space in the center of the castle was called the inner ward. It was enclosed by a high wall called the inner curtain. The area around the outside of the inner curtain was called the outer ward and it was enclosed by a lower wall called the outer curtain. Rounded towers were located along both walls, making it possible for soldiers to observe the entire perimeter of the structure.

Whenever a large doorway was required in either wall it was flanked by a pair of U-shaped towers. The opening itself was fortified by an elaborate system of bridges, gates, and barriers. The whole unit was called a gatehouse. A small gatehouse was located on one side of the outer curtain to protect the postern gate. This gate led to a fortified path running down the side of the outcrop between the castle and the river.

Besides housing Lord Kevin, his family, staff, and servants, when they were in Wales, the castle was to be the permanent home of the steward and his family, their staff and servants, and a garrison of soldiers.

The apartments of both the lord and the steward, along with a chapel, several offices, and a dungeon, were located in the towers of the inner curtain. The rest of the castle's residents lived and worked in buildings in the inner ward.

In planning for the possibility of siege, Master James protected the all important well by locating it in the inner ward. This reduced the danger that the castle's main water supply would ever be poisoned by the enemy — an act which would virtually ensure the castle's defeat. He also included a number of large food-storage rooms throughout the castle, many of which were kept filled at all times.

The outer curtain, which measured about three hundred feet along each of the four sides, was to be twenty feet high and eight feet thick. The walls of the towers would be of the same thickness, but ten feet higher to provide a good view of the curtain on either side. The inner curtain, which measured about two hundred feet to a side, was to be thirty-five feet high and twelve feet thick, and its towers would be fifty feet tall. The increased height of the inner curtain

Inner curtain

would enable soldiers on top of it to fire over and reinforce those soldiers guarding the outer curtain.

The tops of all walls and towers within each curtain were connected by walks. This gave the soldiers on one part of the wall immediate access to any other part that might be under attack. The walk along the tops of the outer curtain was reached by staircases located against its inner face. The walk around the top of the inner curtain was reached by one of the spiral staircases built into each tower. Once on the walk, soldiers were protected by a narrow wall called a battlement, which was built along its outer edge.

Both curtain walls and towers were perfectly vertical, except along the bottom of the outer face, where they spread out at a sharp angle. The sloping base, called a batter, had two main functions. First, it strengthened the structure and, second, it created a surface off which stones and other missiles dropped from the tops of the walls would bounce toward the enemy.

Outer curtain

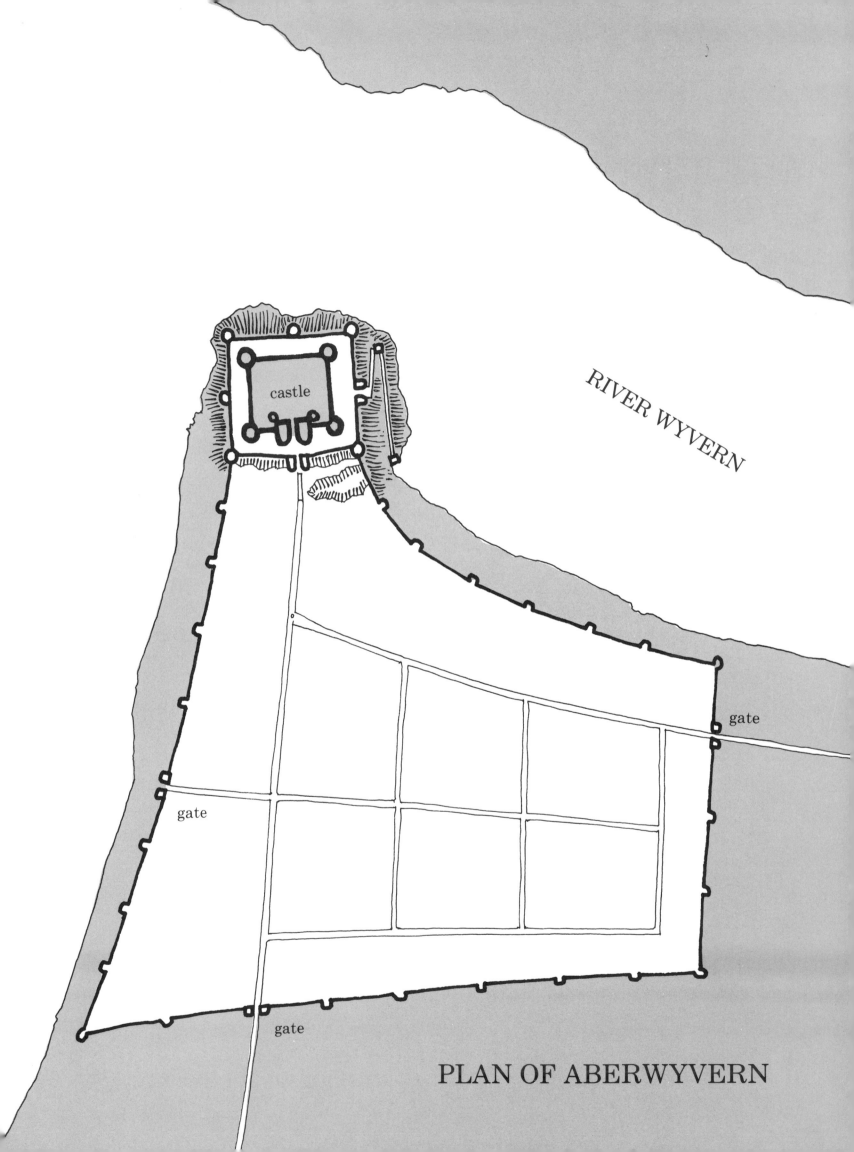

RIVER WYVERN

castle

gate

gate

gate

PLAN OF ABERWYVERN

The plan of the town was drawn next, and it was far less complex. The site was simply divided by a grid of streets into blocks, which were subdivided into lots. On each lot or portion thereof, a settler would build his house, keep his animals, and grow some food. Only English people would be allowed to live in the town at first, and they would be encouraged to do so by the promise of low rent.

Since the only function of the town wall was to protect the town, its design was determined entirely by military considerations. It was to be twenty feet high and five and one-half feet thick and strengthened at intervals of 150 feet by projecting U-shaped towers. A battlemented walk was planned along the top of the wall except where it joined the outer curtain of the castle. There the thickness of the wall was reduced to prevent easy access to the castle. The three entrances into the town were to be fortified by double-towered gatehouses.

Even before the plans were finished, Master James began hiring the necessary labor. He sent word to the constables of several English cities indicating the numbers and types of workers required. At the height of the work, the project would require over three thousand people, including quarriers, stone masons,

Master James

Quarrymen

A Master Mason

Carpenters

mortar makers, carpenters, blacksmiths, plumbers, diggers, and an assortment of laborers. Each discipline was to be overseen by one or more master craftsmen, who in turn would be responsible to Master James.

A Blacksmith

A Mortar Maker and Carrier

Diggers

Master James's Dog

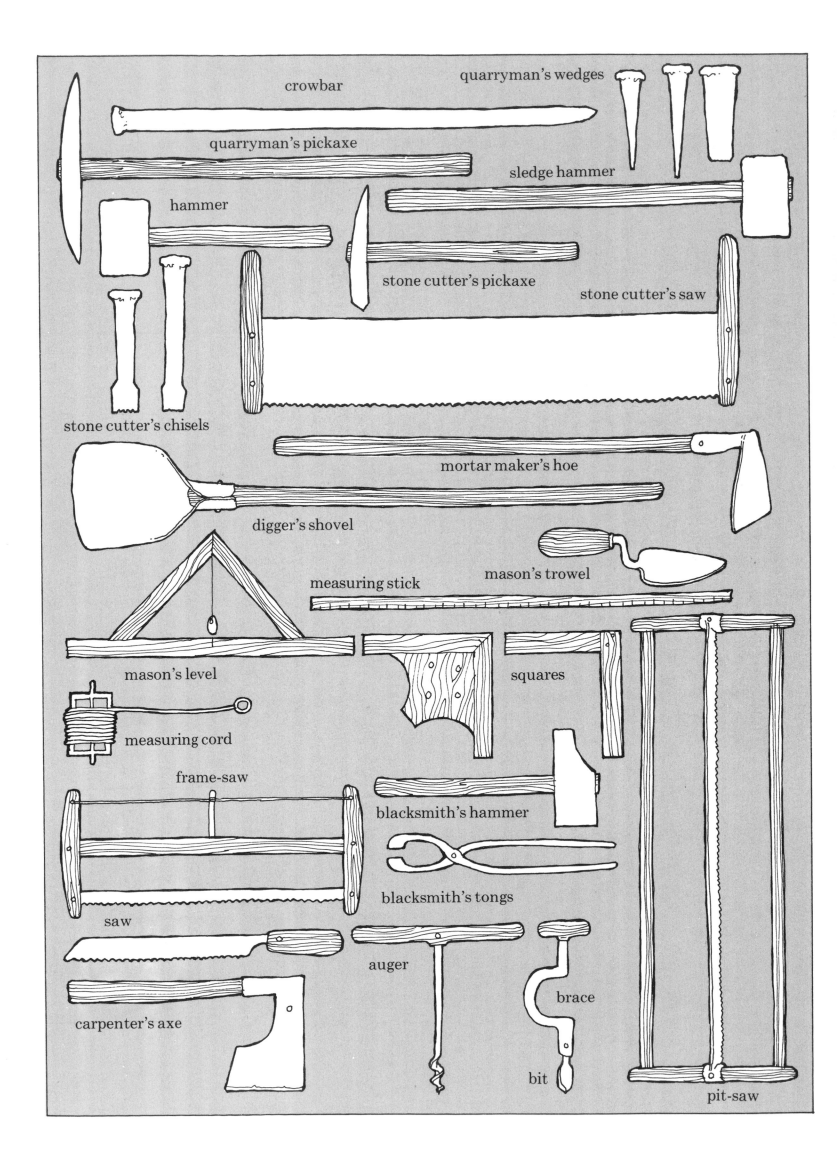

In addition to planning for the workmen, he ordered a great many tools. Most of the tools, whether for working stone or wood, were made of iron and could be repaired in one of the blacksmith shops.

Shortly after Lord Kevin's arrival the plans were approved, and on June 8, 1283, Master James and his surveyors began marking off the locations of all the main walls and towers on the site. Because of its location on the outcrop, the castle required no special foundations, and laborers began roughly leveling the areas that the building was to occupy.

Not all of the town wall, on the other hand, would rest on rock. Parts of it required a deep foundation to reduce the chance of uneven settlement and cracking. Many of the diggers were put to work excavating the foundation holes along the inside of the town ditch.

Another group was assigned to the outcrop to dig the well and to cut a trench or moat across the landward side of the rock. This would increase the security of the castle site by reducing access to it from the town.

While Master James supervised work on the project, Lord Kevin began collecting the money to pay for it. Some of the money would come from rent and taxes to be paid by farmers in the surrounding villages. They automatically became Lord Kevin's tenants when he was given the land on which they lived and worked. To ensure that all due amounts would be collected, Walter of Ipswich, the lord's bailiff, was dispatched to the surrounding countryside with a contingent of soldiers to determine the population and record their holdings. The rest of the money would come either from the sale of livestock and produce raised on Kevin's land in both England and Wales, or directly from his personal funds.

By mid-July the first cartloads of local sandstone had arrived from a nearby quarry. Work began simultaneously on the outer curtain wall and the foundations of the town wall. The mortar used to bind the stones together was a mixture of water, sand, and lime. The inner and outer faces of each wall were constructed first. The stones were carefully fitted and mortared in horizontal layers called courses. When a height of three or four feet was reached, the space between these two narrow walls was completely filled with rubble — a mixture of stones and mortar.

Master masons continually checked both the vertical and horizontal accuracy of the walls as they grew. Every so often, a course of slate was laid, creating a more precise horizontal bed on which to build the next few feet.

As the height of the walls increased, a temporary wooden framework, called scaffolding, was required to support both workers and materials. The poles were lashed together and secured to the wall by horizontal pieces set into holes, called putlog holes, which were intentionally left between the stones. The putlog holes along the outer face of both walls and towers rose on a gradual incline. Planks were nailed to the scaffolding inserted in these holes to create ramps up which heavy material could be dragged or carried.

Hoists and pulleys were attached to the scaffolding for lifting lighter materials and tools.

When a section of castle or town wall reached walk level, its battlement or crenelation was constructed. This was a wall consisting of alternating high and low segments. The high segments, called merlons, each contained an arrow loop — a narrow vertical slit through which a soldier could shoot his arrows

and remain completely protected. The lower segments, called embrasures, created openings from which missiles could be dropped on the enemy.

Every merlon was capped by three vertical stone spikes called finials, and immediately below each arrow loop was a square putlog hole. In time of battle, beams or logs were extended through these holes to support a temporary wooden balcony or hoarding from which missiles and arrows could be dropped and fired more accurately toward the base of the walls.

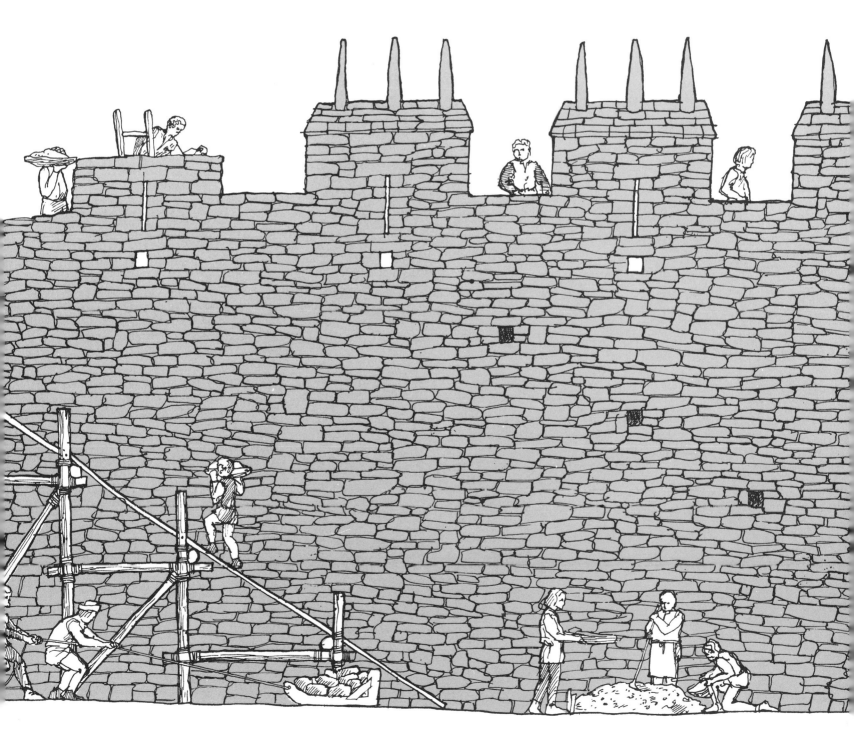

In December construction was halted because the low temperatures tended
to crack the wet mortar. After protecting the tops of the unfinished walls with

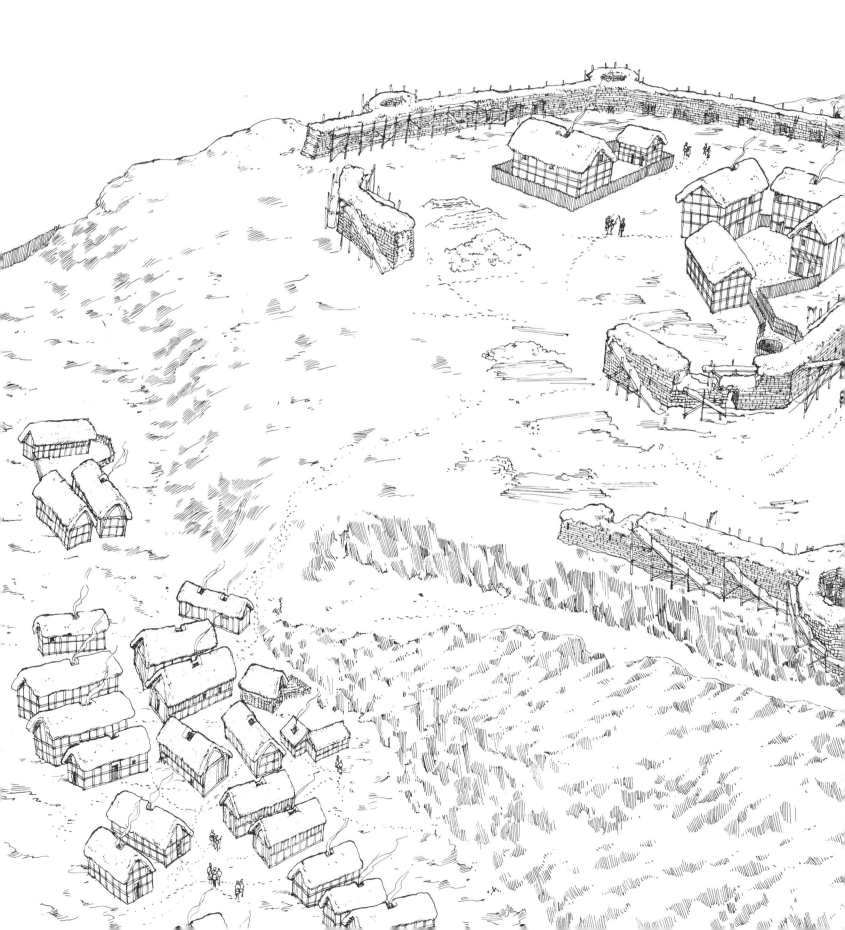

a covering of straw and dung, many of the workers returned to England for the rest of the winter.

The few hundred that remained worked in the sheds preparing material and equipment for the resumption of work in the spring.

By the end of the following March most of the workers had returned and work picked up exactly where it had left off. As each length of foundation for the town wall was finished, work began on the wall itself. Master James had planned the wall as a series of connected but independent sections.

Wooden bridges, located at wall-walk level behind each tower, were the only means of getting from one section to another. In the event that a portion of the wall was overrun, the defenders simply removed the bridges at each end of that segment, forcing the enemy either to come down the exposed stairway against the inner face of the wall or to go back the way they came.

The two most common openings in the castle walls were windows and arrow loops. Behind each opening a recess was cut into the thickness of the wall. The recess behind an arrow loop was a vertical wedge-shaped space designed to give the archer more flexibility in aiming his bow.

Because the windows were the only source of natural light, the recesses

behind them were often the size of small rooms and contained built-in window seats along each side.

For security reasons the windows near the bottom of walls and towers were very narrow, whereas those at the top were quite wide. All the windows were protected by an iron grille and could be closed off by wooden shutters. In the living quarters the windows were also fitted with glass.

Throughout the summer and autumn work progressed without interruption, and by the end of the season of 1284 several of the towers and adjacent sections of town wall had reached wall-walk height.

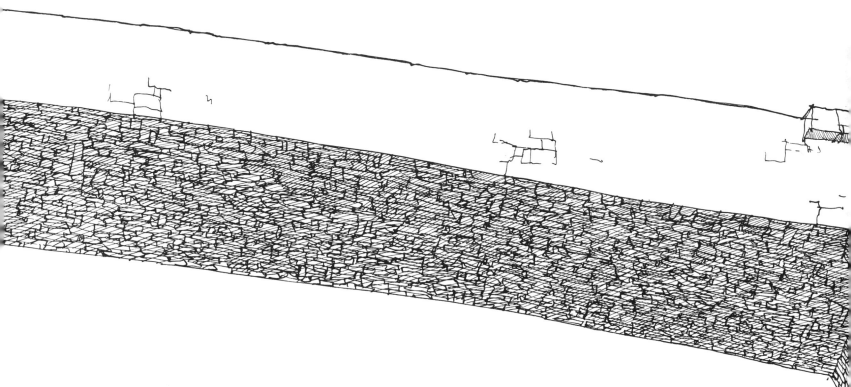

The following March one hundred extra masons arrived with the returning workers to speed up progress on the inner curtain and its towers. To increase the defensive strength of the already massive inner curtain, Master James designed its towers so that each could be sealed off and defended independently of the rest of the wall. There were only two entrances to a tower. The first was at the base and opened into the inner ward. The second was at the top and could be reached only from the wall walk. In the event that the inner ward was overrun, both openings could be secured by heavy wooden doors.

Each tower contained three rooms, one above the other, connected by a spiral staircase built into the thickness of the tower wall. The spiral staircase continued above the level of the tower walk to the top of the turret.

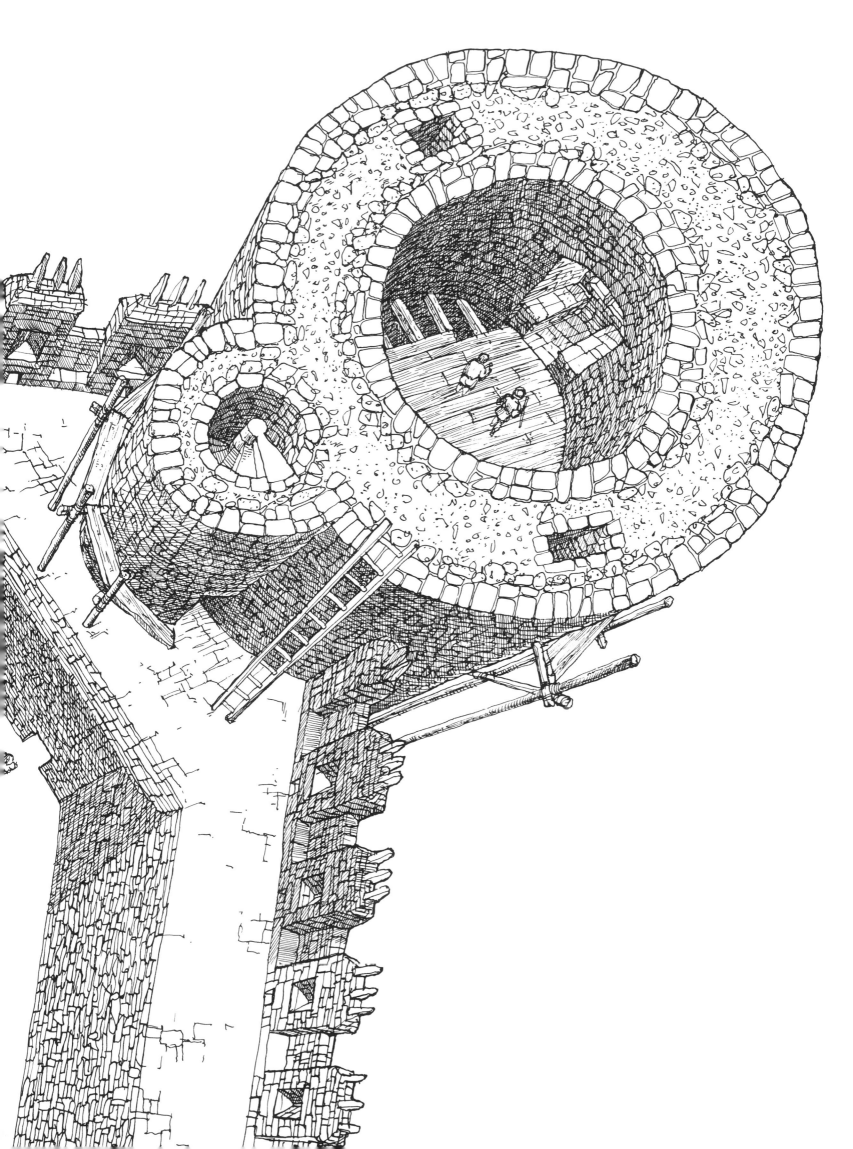

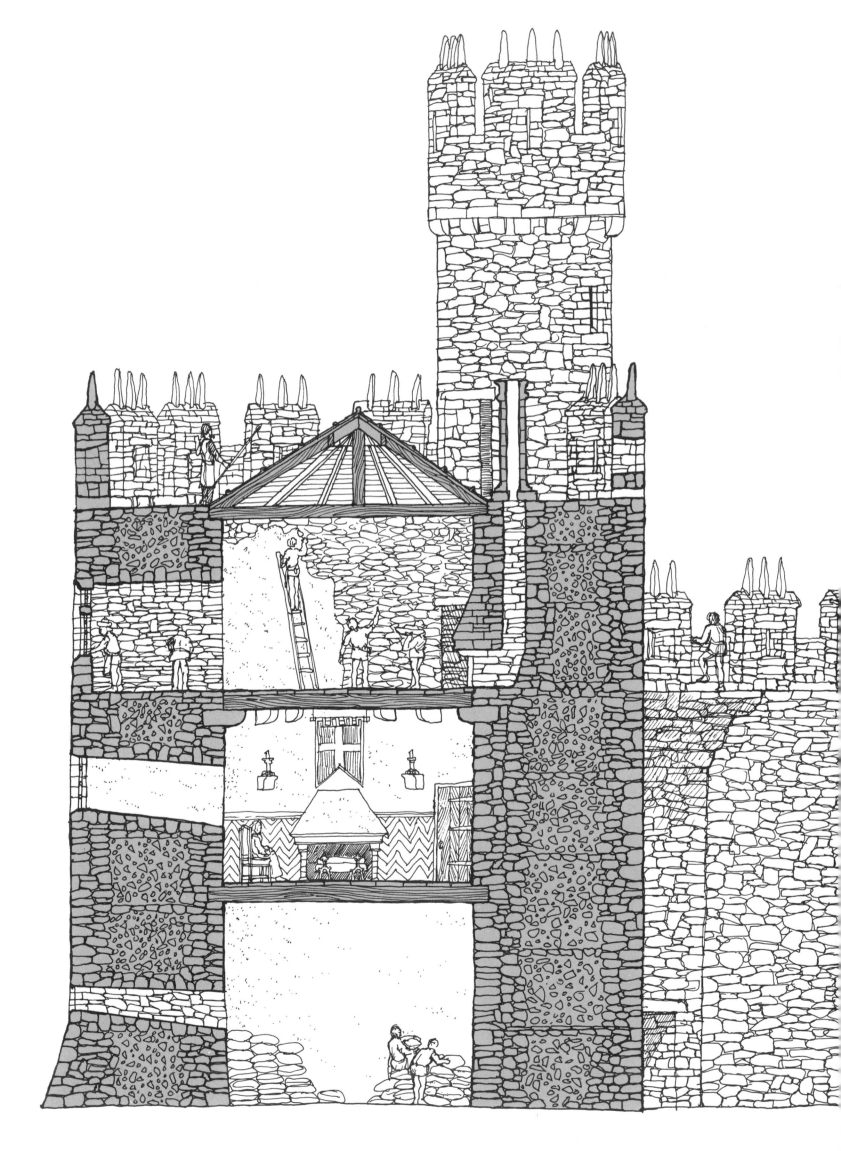

The room at ground level, called the basement, was usually used for storage, enabling a tower to be self-sufficient during a siege. The upper rooms were used either as office or living space. All the floors, except that of the basement, which was the rock itself, were made of wooden planks nailed to heavy oak beams which spanned the interior of each tower at the required height. The beams were either inserted into the wall during construction or were supported by projecting blocks of stone called corbels.

The opening at the top of each tower was capped by a conical timber roof. The roof beams or rafters were set into a groove around the inside edge of the tower walk and covered with either sheets of lead or slate tiles.

Once the roof of a tower was sealed against the rain, the rooms below were finished. Each of the upper rooms was to be heated by its own fireplace, which was built into the wall during construction. Vertical shafts, called flues, were also built into the walls to draw the smoke from the fireplaces up to chimneys on the tower walks.

During the day almost all light came from the windows, and at night oil lamps and candles were required to supplement the light from the fireplace. They were usually placed on corbels set into the walls around the room. The walls of the rooms were covered with a thick coat of plaster and either painted, covered with painted cloth hangings, or both. All the floors, including that of the basement, were covered with reeds and sweet-smelling herbs which were swept out and replaced every month.

By October of 1285 the outer curtain was finished except for the gatehouses, and many of the masons were assigned to work on the last two corner towers of the inner curtain.

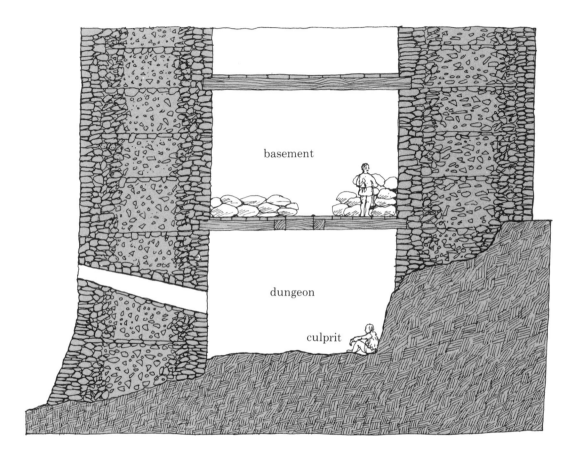

In one tower, where the level of the outcrop was slightly lower than in the rest of the inner ward, a room was cut into the rock below the basement to serve as a jail or dungeon. It could only be reached through a trapdoor in the basement floor. The light in the dungeon came through a narrow slit cut into the thickness of the wall.

The one tower that was completely different from the rest was the chapel tower. Instead of having two rooms above the basement it contained one room that was two stories high. The apse or altar area of the chapel was built into a large window recess. The stone window frame was carefully cut and fitted with pieces of colorful stained glass. Directly across the chapel from the apse a second recess was cut into the tower wall but this time on the second-story level. From this space Lord Kevin and his family would observe the services while the rest of the worshipers stood on the wooden floor below.

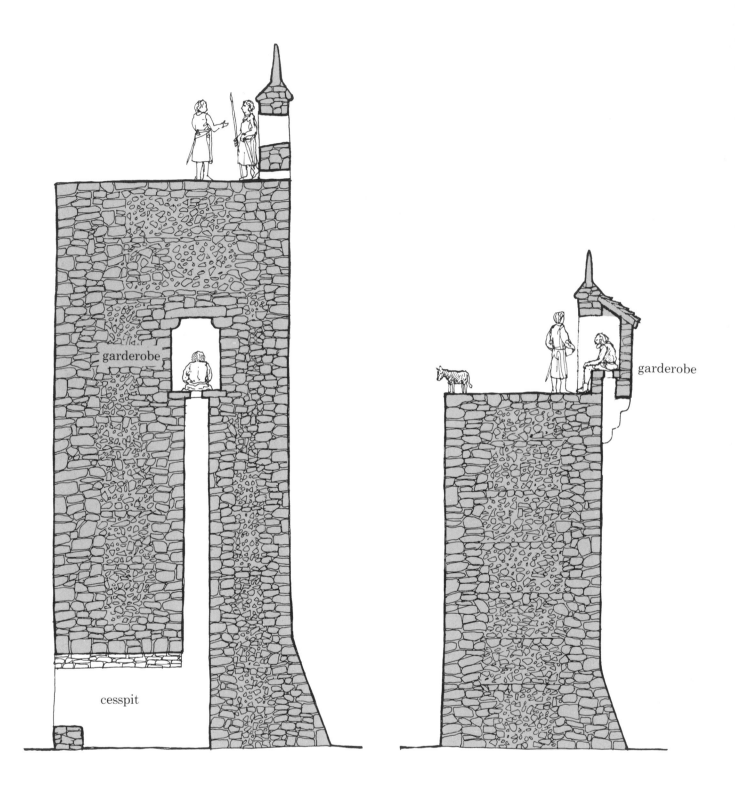

The castle's many toilets, called garderobes, were located in the curtain walls and were reached by narrow passages. Each garderobe was lit by a small window or arrow loop. The seat was simply a slab of stone with a round hole cut in it. Along the outer curtain the seat was supported on corbels and projected

out beyond the face of the wall. The garderobes of the inner curtain were often grouped together over vertical shafts either within the wall or built against it. These led to a cesspit at the foot of the wall which had to be periodically cleaned out.

TOWN GATEHOUSE SECTION

The last major pieces of construction in both castle and town defense were the gatehouses. Because these were the most vulnerable parts of the walls, they were designed and built with great care.

Between the two towers of each gatehouse, a row of parallel stone arches supported a room above the road. From this room a heavy timber grille called a portcullis could be lowered to block the opening. The portcullis slid up and down in grooves cut into the walls on both sides. The bottom of each vertical piece of the portcullis was pointed and capped with iron. The face of the portcullis was also clad with iron for additional strength. Beyond the portcullis was a set of heavy wooden doors also reinforced with iron straps. Immediately behind the doors were two holes opposite each other in the walls. A heavy piece of timber called a drawbar was pulled from the basement through one of the two holes, across the roadway, and set into the other hole to further secure the doors.

Arrow loops in the basements of the towers gave the soldiers complete control of the entry area.

If any part of an enemy force was careless enough to get caught in the space between the towers, it was showered with a variety of missiles and arrows. These would be dropped or fired through openings in the floor above called murder holes.

By the end of 1286 the town wall was almost finished. As the security of the town increased so did its population. In addition to the farmers who worked the land outside the walls, many of Aberwyvern's settlers were merchants and craftsmen and their families. They built their houses very close together to

maintain as much grazing and planting land as possible within the walls. Since there were no sidewalks, the building fronts were lined up right along the unpaved streets.

The first houses were built close to the public well, but eventually houses spread along all the streets.

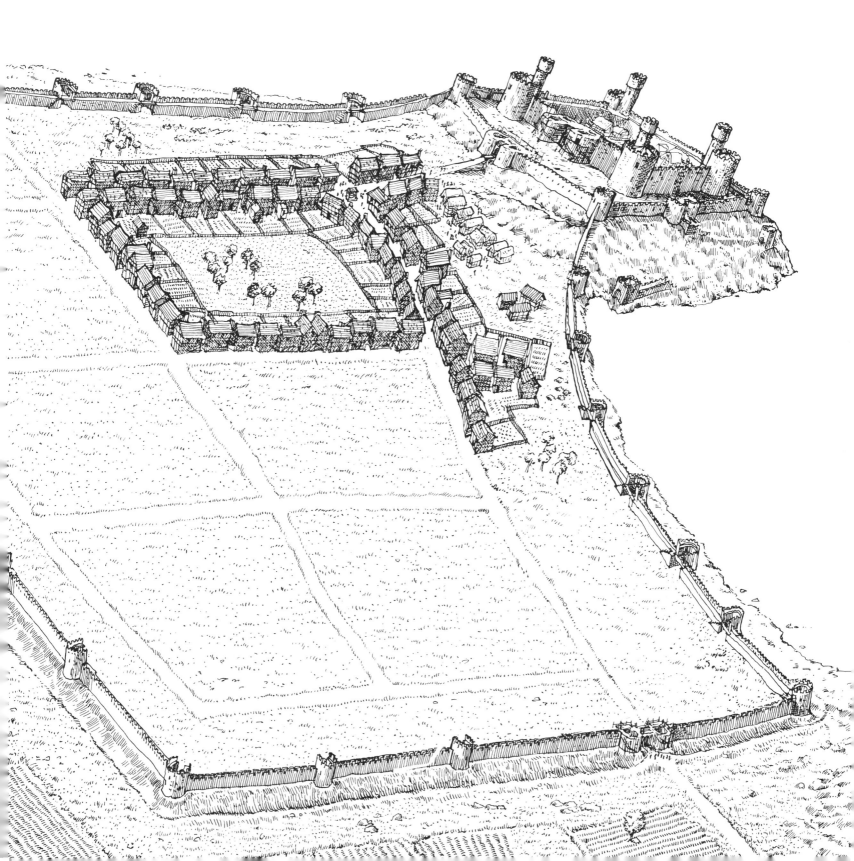

All the houses were of half-timber construction. This meant that the main structure consisted of wooden beams, usually oak, and the spaces between the timbers were filled with wattle and daub. Wattle was a mat of woven sticks and reeds and daub was the mud or clay smeared on to strengthen and seal it. The roofs were covered with either slate tiles or wooden shingles.

The ground floor was beaten or packed earth, and all the floors were covered with a layer of reeds. Heat was provided by a single fireplace, which also had to light the room since the window openings were generally very small and usually covered with oiled sheep or goat skin.

Most of Aberwyvern's businessmen, like Thomas the master shoemaker and Oliver the master tailor, manufactured and sold their wares from their homes. Their workrooms and shops were located at the front of their houses on the ground floor. During the daytime, horizontal wooden shutters were opened out toward the street. The bottom one dropped down to serve as a counter on which items could be displayed, while the top shutter swung upwards and served as an awning. Shops selling such things as produce, fish, and wine were often located near the gates through which those commodities were delivered.

When the population of Aberwyvern reached several hundred, the town was granted the status of parish and given a priest.

Shortly after his arrival the priest began supervising the building of a church on a piece of land donated by Lord Kevin. It was the only stone building within the town and soon became both a visual and a social focal point for the community. The gratitude of the townspeople for the church was clearly shown by the fact that much of the labor was either freely given or paid for by generous contributions — no small sacrifice for people already working seven days a week.

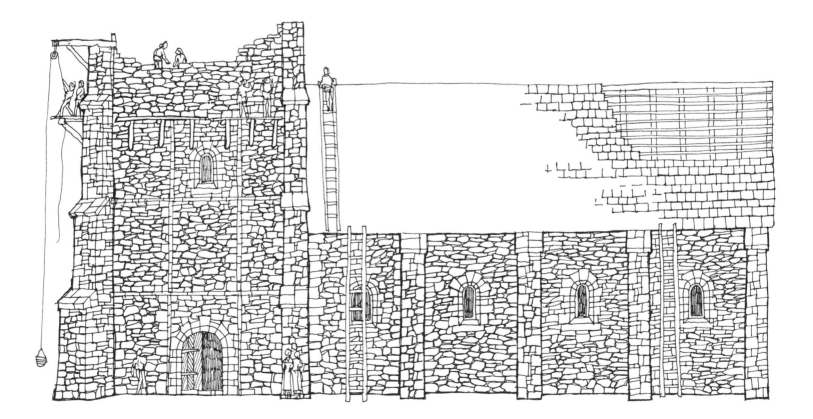

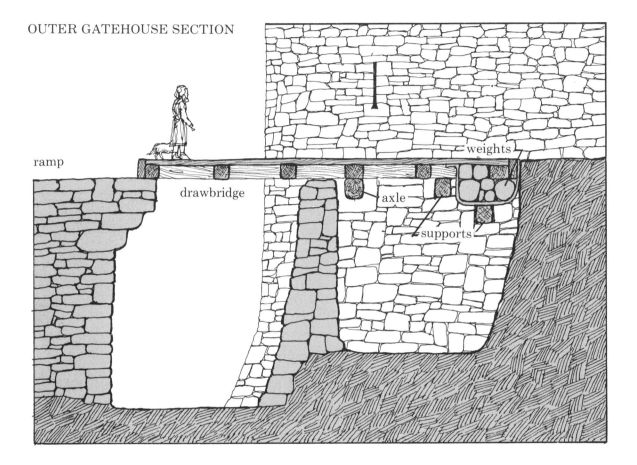

OUTER GATEHOUSE SECTION

ramp

drawbridge

weights

axle

supports

During the summer of 1287 work was completed on the gatehouses leading into the castle. The inner gatehouse had two portcullises, two sets of doors, and two drawbars. The outer gatehouse was equally well equipped and had the additional advantage of a drawbridge.

This flat timber platform was designed to pivot on an axle like a seesaw. The axle was set into holes cut in the base of each tower on both sides of the opening. The bridge was then fastened to the top of the axle — one end extending in through the gateway toward the outer ward, the other end spanning the moat. The inner end of the bridge was weighted and when the supports were removed it swung down into a specially designed pit cut into the rock between the towers. At the same time the other end swung upward, breaking the connection across the moat and blocking the entrance. To allow entry, the bridge would then be hoisted back into a horizontal position and the supports replaced underneath the weighted end.

The drawbridge connected the castle to the end of a twenty-five-foot-high stone ramp. Anyone wishing to enter the castle would have to climb the ramp and then be exposed to attack by the soldiers along the walls.

The postern gatehouse was also finished at this time and it too had a drawbridge.

Once the gatehouses were finished work began on the buildings of the now secure inner ward. The first of the temporary buildings to be replaced was the structure that housed the garrison.

The new building had two stories and was of half-timber construction with a slate roof. While the second floor served as the living quarters for the men, the basement was divided between stables and storage rooms. One of the storage rooms contained many of the garrison's weapons, all of which had been brought from England. Any necessary repairs to the weapons were the responsibility of the blacksmith, whose shop stood at the end of the barracks.

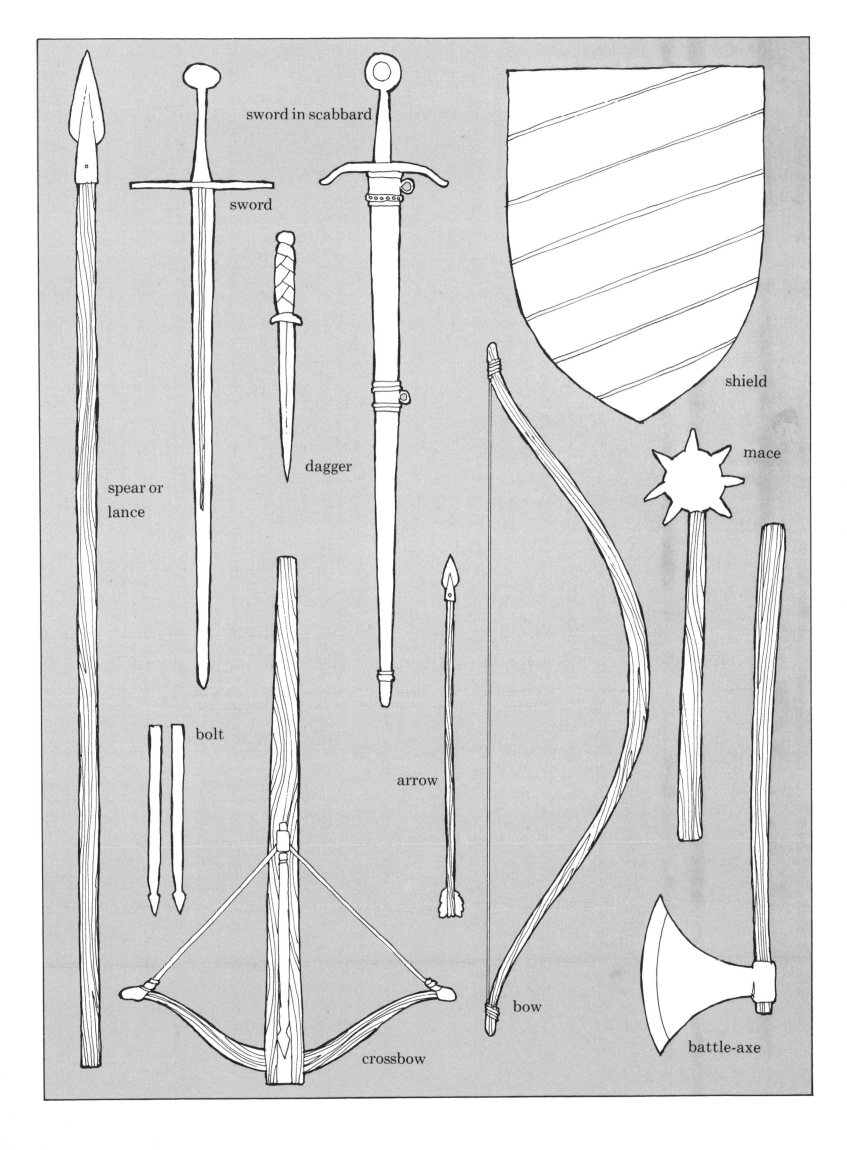

spear or lance

sword

sword in scabbard

dagger

shield

mace

bolt

arrow

bow

crossbow

battle-axe

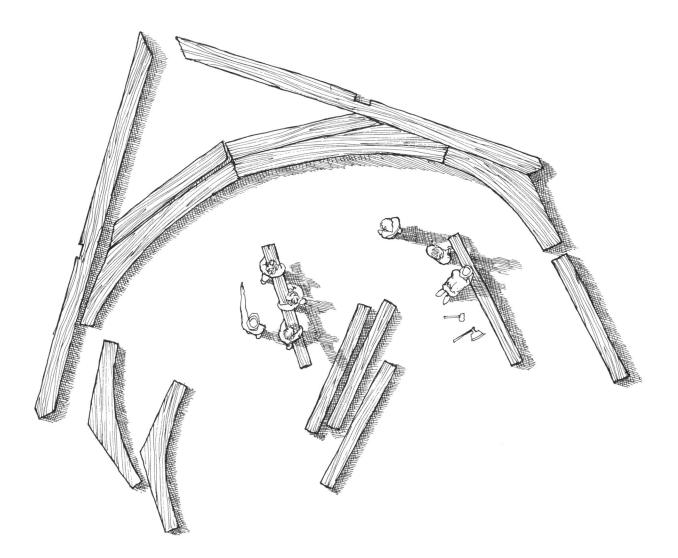

The largest new building in the ward was to be the great hall. It would serve as the general gathering and dining area for the entire population of the castle, it would be thirty-five feet wide and over one hundred feet long.

Master James located the hall in one corner of the inner ward so that only two new walls would be needed to enclose the space. They were both built of stone and capped with battlements. The longer of the two ran parallel to the rear curtain wall and contained three large windows and a door. The new wall at the end of the hall contained a large fireplace and a doorway to the kitchen. Two other fireplaces were already built into the curtain walls. The masons had set a row of corbels into the rear curtain wall about eight feet off the floor. This was repeated in the longer of the new walls.

As soon as the walls were finished, the carpenters began work on the roof. It was to rest on a row of parallel timber frames called trusses, which would span the width of the hall. Each truss was arched on the bottom for additional strength and built to form a peak on top.

First a vertical wooden post was set on each corbel and secured to the wall. Next, the carefully cut pieces of timber were assembled and hoisted into place with the ends of each truss resting on opposite wall posts. The tops of the trusses were then connected to each other and covered with wood planks and lead sheets. Once the roof was watertight the interior walls were plastered and painted and the windows were filled with glass.

Next to the hall and in the other rear corner of the inner ward was the kitchen. It contained ovens for baking bread, special fireplaces for cooking and smoking meat, and a large storage area for wine and ale barrels. Set into the rear curtain wall was a large stone sink. Water was piped directly into the sink from a stone tank called a cistern located at the top of the corner tower. The flat sloping roof over the kitchen was supported on beams set into a row of holes in the rear curtain.

New half-timber buildings were eventually constructed around the edge of the entire inner ward, replacing the last of the laborers' housing and workshops built almost four years earlier. They contained not only additional living space for Lord Kevin, Lady Catherine, and their closest attendants, but also a number of guest rooms and private quarters for members of the staff, including Walter the bailiff, Robert the Chaplain, and Lionel the barber and doctor.

Smaller rooms on the ground floors of all the buildings were allotted to servants, laborers, and general storage. Master John, the castle cook, lived in a small apartment close to the kitchen with his family and two assistants. In another corner of the ward kennels were built, along with a special shed called a mew, in which Lord Kevin's hunting birds were housed.

Although a number of dogs and cats were allowed to roam at will throughout the castle in hopes of controlling the rodent population, one small area of the inner ward was intentionally fenced off. Here Lady Catherine had insisted that a lawn of imported English turf be laid and a garden for flowers and herbs be planted.

In October of 1288, when the walls and towers of the castle were finished, the exterior of the entire structure was whitewashed with lime, giving it the appearance of having been carved from a single enormous piece of stone and greatly enhancing its already powerful image.

The following spring saw only a handful of laborers returning to Aberwyvern.

There was very little left to do, and the day-to-day maintenance of castle and town wall could now be managed by the craftsmen who had settled permanently in the town. At this point Lady Catherine considered the castle ready for occupation and, on April 29, arrived with her ladies in waiting, children, and servants to join Lord Kevin in their Welsh home.

Two years later, in an attempt to encourage further settlement, Lord Kevin granted Aberwyvern a charter. This relieved the residents of the town, present and future, of paying certain taxes, which Kevin could afford to dispense with, now that the castle was finished. It also gave the residents the right to elect a mayor and town council, to establish their own court for minor crimes, and to hold a weekly market along the main street.

By 1294, Kevin's castle overlooked a thriving yet still not overcrowded community, and in December of that year King Edward, while en route to one of his own castles, paid a visit. On the day of his arrival all the shops and businesses closed down as the entire population lined the riverbank to catch a glimpse of the royal ships.

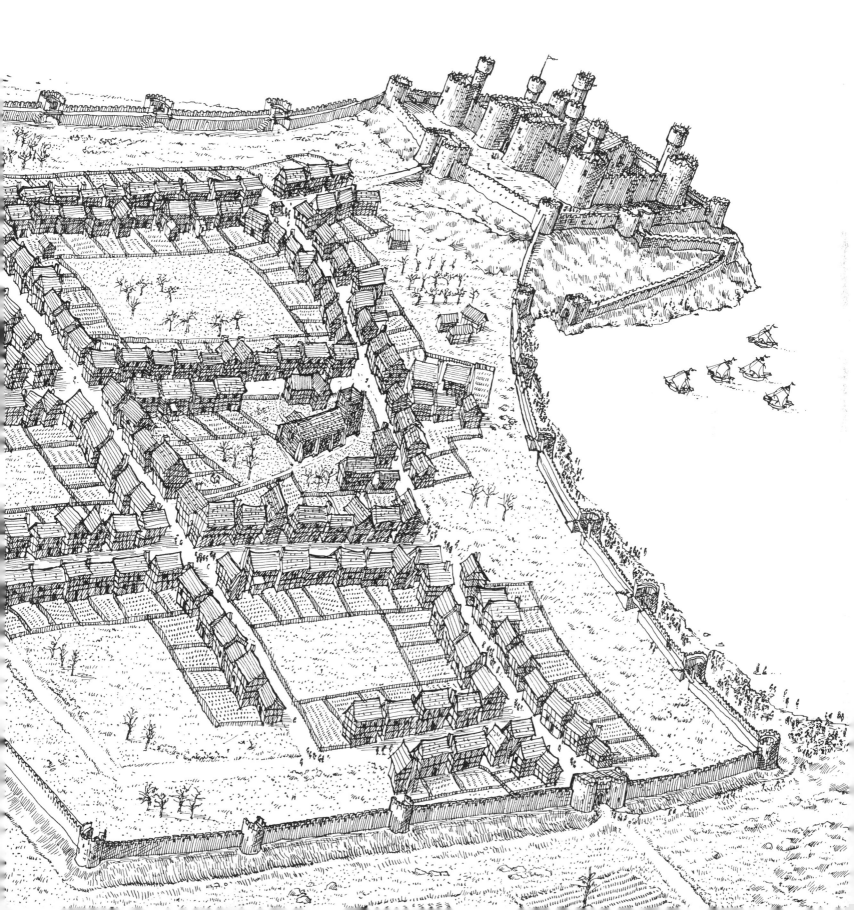

That evening a dinner was held at the castle to which the mayor, the council, and several of the town's prominent merchants were invited. The walls of the great hall were specially hung with colorful banners, and a fresh covering of reeds was spread over the floor. The king and his ministers sat with Lord Kevin and Lady Catherine behind a long table on a raised platform at one end of the hall. Everyone else sat at tables set up on the floor close to the walls. Food and drink flowed continuously from Master John's kitchen and entertainment was provided by a variety of musicians, acrobats, and jugglers. The festivities went on into the early morning hours, long after the king had retired.

Edward was not in Wales for social reasons, however. He had come to quell an outbreak of rebellions led by several Welsh princes. Before leaving Aberwyvern, he warned Lord Kevin about the situation and encouraged him to prepare for any eventuality. Since Master James had virtually secured the town against direct military attack, most of the effort went into preparations for defense against a possible siege. During the next few months, therefore, extra large quantities of food and grain were stored away in every available building and room in both castle and town, including the church. A large number of arrows were made, boulders were collected for dropping off the walls, and as an extra precaution the hoardings were installed around the tops of all the walls and towers.

Beginning on April 11, 1295, both Master James's defense and the preparations of all the town residents were put to the test. Hundreds of Welsh soldiers under Prince Daffyd of Gwynedd circled the town. Several ships were anchored around the castle to prevent the delivery of supplies or escape by water. By the end of June most of the buildings outside the town walls including a flour mill, barns, and several farmhouses had been destroyed, along with much of the farmland. Supplies within the town, however, were holding up well, and no real progress had been made by either side.

Upon hearing that a large English force was moving down from the north as part of a general campaign to crush all the rebellions, Prince Daffyd ordered a direct attack. A large number of catapults were assembled and aimed at both the town and the castle.

Each of these heavy timber weapons was outfitted with an arm which could be drawn back under great pressure. When the pressure was released, the arm would shoot forward, flinging a variety of missiles either against the walls or over them.

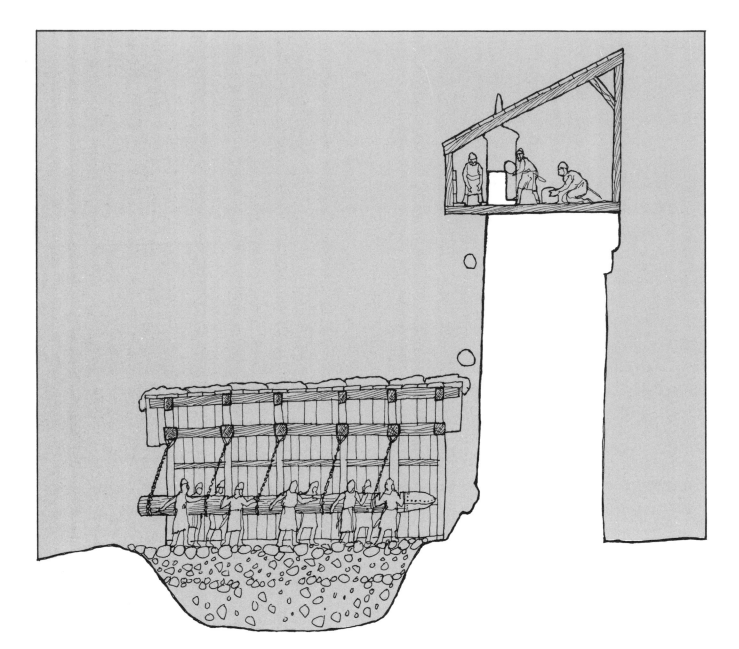

In addition to the aerial bombardment, Prince Daffyd initiated a series of more direct assaults on the walls. Under cover of darkness Welsh soldiers filled the ditch at several locations around the town wall with earth, stones, and logs.

A prefabricated shed was then erected at the foot of the wall. It was covered with animal pelts and earth to reduce the chances of its being set on fire by burning arrows from above. Inside the shed a thick tree trunk was hung by chains from beams under the roof. This was called a battering ram; one end of it was shaped to a point and capped with iron. The pointed end was aimed at the wall and the battering ram was then rocked back and forth by a team of soldiers.

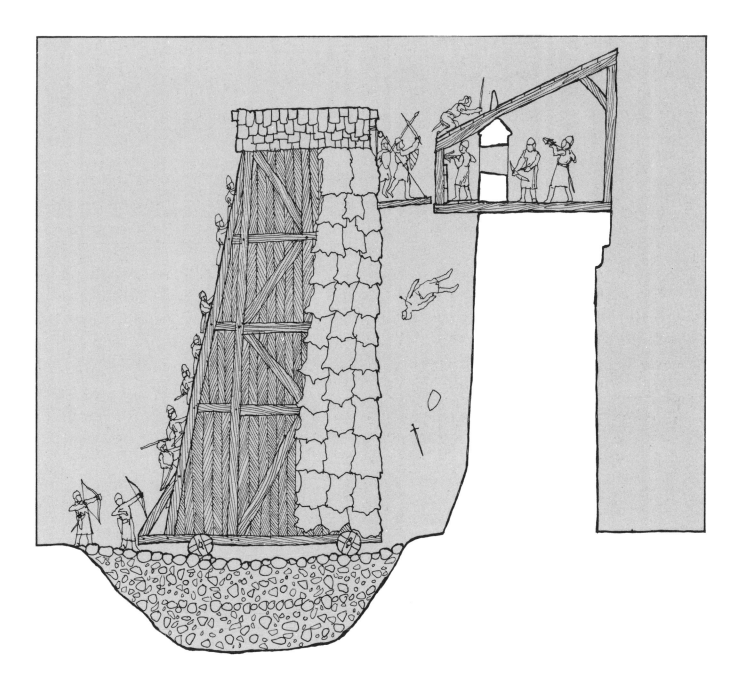

Meanwhile, a second group of soldiers had rolled a tall wooden structure, called a siege tower, over another part of the ditch and into position next to the hoardings. They then climbed up the rear of the tower to a platform on top, from which they lowered a small drawbridge and attempted to cross over onto the wall. After two hours of fierce hand-to-hand combat the Welsh withdrew. Their tower had been set ablaze by the defenders.

For almost a week one attempt after another was initiated against the walls.

During this time another group of attackers had been hard at work. They were called sappers and it was their job to dig a tunnel, called a mine, under the wall. It was supported by a framework of logs. When the tunnel extended far enough under the wall the framework was burned, causing the wall above to collapse. The sappers worked around the clock, protected by a wooden shed called a sapper's tent which was pushed against the wall. It too was covered in an attempt to make it fireproof. The sappers were reinforced by archers, who stood behind movable wooden screens and fired at the hoardings along the wall.

When news reached Prince Daffyd that the English were only a few days away, he ordered the mine set on fire. It was filled with dry wood and straw and fueled with several dead pigs. The fire roared for hours, as water was desperately poured from the hoardings. But it eventually became obvious to both sides that the wall was too strong and the tunnel not large enough to cause its collapse. Facing not only defeat but probable annihilation, the prince ordered his men to retreat.

Master James's defenses had done their job well, but, as King Edward had realized from the start, no amount of military architecture or number of soldiers would ever conquer the people of Wales. They would have to be encouraged to give up the fight on their own.

In the months following the uprising, several Welsh families, from the surrounding countryside, tired of the bloodshed and interested in sharing Aberwyvern's obvious advantages, were encouraged to settle along the roads outside the gates. On market days and during fairs they were allowed into the town to

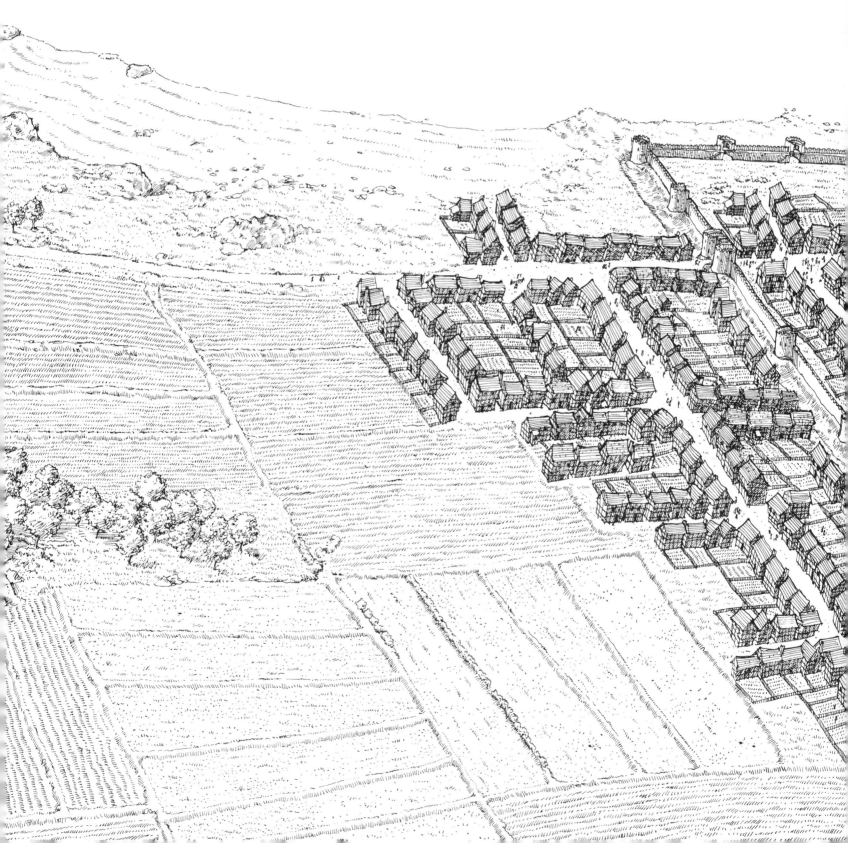

sell their products and buy those available within the walls. As time passed the population outside the walls grew, and with it all kinds of buildings took shape. Eventually a whole network of streets and alleys wrapped itself around the walls and Aberwyvern became a town within a town.

The "conquest" of Wales was only complete when both English and Welsh passed freely through gates into towns like Aberwyvern, building their houses and observing their individual customs side by side. Thus Edward's victory wasn't really achieved until almost two hundred years after his death.

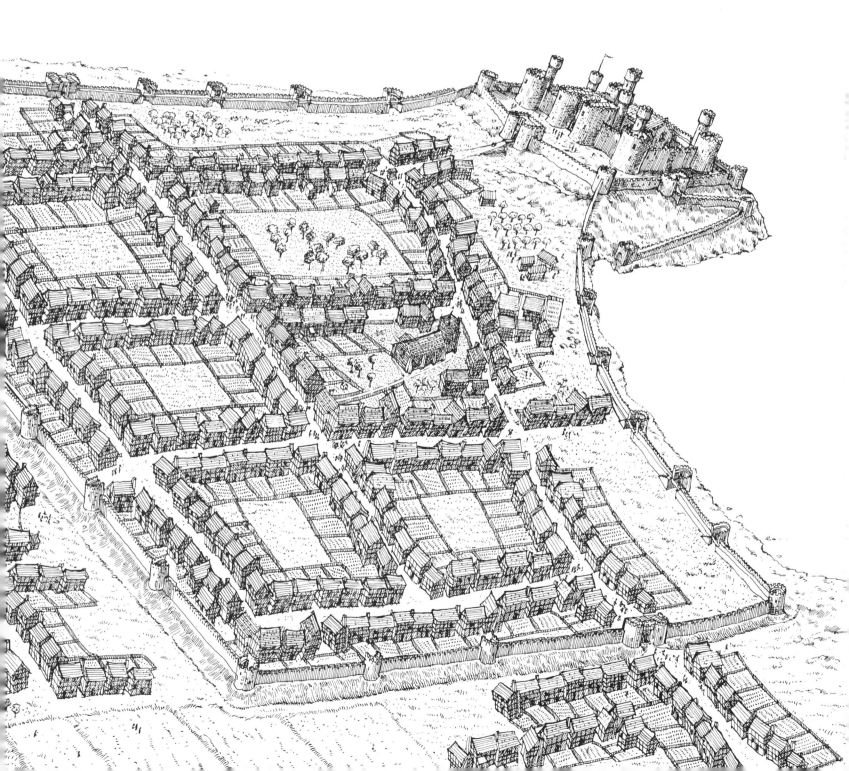

By that time Master James's mighty castle stood partially roofless and completely neglected except as a quarry for new buildings, and his once impressive town wall was now more of a nuisance to the town fathers than a necessity.

GLOSSARY

ARROW LOOP
A narrow vertical slit cut into a wall through which arrows could be fired from the inside.

BATTER
The sharp angle at the base of all the walls and towers along their exterior surface.

BATTLEMENT
A narrow wall built along the outer edge of the wall walk to protect the soldiers against attack.

CESSPIT
The opening in a wall in which the waste from one or more garderobes was collected.

CORBEL
A projecting block of stone built into a wall during construction.

CRENELATION
Battlement.

DAUB
A mud or clay mixture applied over wattle to strengthen and seal it.

DRAWBRIDGE
A heavy timber platform built to span a moat between gatehouse and surrounding land that could be raised when required to block the entrance.

DUNGEON
The jail, usually found in one of the towers.

EMBRASURE
The low segment of the alternating high and low segments of a battlement.

FINIAL
A slender vertical piece of stone used to decorate the tops of the merlons.

FOUNDATION
The underground construction required to prevent the uneven settlement of a wall when bedrock is too far below the surface.

GARDEROBE
A small latrine or toilet either built into the thickness of a wall or projected out from it.

GATEHOUSE
The complex of towers, bridges, and barriers built to protect each entrance through a castle or town wall.

GREAT HALL
The building in the inner ward that housed the main meeting and dining area for the castle's residents.

HALF-TIMBER
The most common form of medieval construction in which walls were made of a wood frame structure filled with wattle and daub.

HOARDING
A temporary wooden balcony suspended from the tops of walls and towers before a battle, from which missiles and arrows could be dropped and fired accurately toward the bases of the walls.

INNER CURTAIN
The high wall that surrounds the inner ward.

INNER WARD
The open area in the center of a castle.

MERLON
The high segment of the alternating high and low segments of a battlement.

MOAT
A deep trench dug around a castle to prevent access from the surrounding land. It could either be left dry or filled with water.

MORTAR
A mixture of sand, water, and lime used to bind stones together permanently.

OUTER CURTAIN
The wall that encloses the outer ward.

OUTER WARD
The area around the outside of and adjacent to the inner curtain.

PALISADE
A sturdy wooden fence usually built to enclose a site until a permanent stone wall can be constructed.

PORTCULLIS
A heavy timber grille that could be raised or lowered between the towers of each gatehouse to open or close the passage.

POSTERN GATE
A side or less important gate into a castle.

PUTLOG HOLE
A hole intentionally left in the surface of a wall for the insertion of a horizontal pole.

RUBBLE
A random mixture of rocks and mortar.

SCAFFOLDING
The temporary wooden framework built next to a wall to support both workers and materials.

SIEGE
The military tactic that involves the surrounding and isolation of a castle, town, or army by another army until the trapped forces are starved into surrender.

STEWARD
The man responsible for running the day-to-day affairs of the castle in the absence of the lord.

TRUSS
One of the timber frames built to support the roof over the great hall.

TURRET
A small tower rising above and resting on one of the main towers, usually used as a lookout point.

WALL WALK
The area along the tops of the walls from which soldiers defended both castle and town.

WATTLE
A mat of woven sticks and weeds.